J.M.W. Turner

Alix Wood

W

FRANKLIN WATTS

LONDON • SYDNEY

Franklin Watts

First published in Great Britain in 2015 by the Watts Publishing Group

Copyright © Alix Wood Books
Produced for Franklin Watts by Alix Wood Books www.alixwoodbooks.co.uk

Editor: Eloise Macgregor
Designer: Alix Wood

Photo Credits: Cover, 1, 4 top, 7, 8, 12 © Tate Britain; 3, 26 © Shutterstock; 4 bottom,
5 © public domain; 9 top © nga/Rosenwald Collection; 9 bottom © Turner Contemporary,
Margate; 6 © Indianapolis Museum of Art; 10, 11, 27 © Yale Center for British Art;
12-13 © nga/Widener Collection; 14, 15, 16-17, 18-19 © National Gallery, London;
20-21 © John Paul Getty Museum; 22 © Metropolitan Museum of Art, New York;
23 © The Fuller Foundation; 24 © Cleveland Museum of Art; 25 top © nga/Timken
Collection; 25 bottom © Jialing Gao; 28 © Sheffield Museum; 29 © Tokyo Fuji Art Museum

Dewey number 709

ISBN 978 1 4451 4419 1

Library eBook ISBN 978 1 4451 4420 7

Printed in China

Franklin Watts
An imprint of
Hachette Children's Group
Part of The Watts Publishing Group
Carmelite House
50 Victoria Embankment
London EC4Y 0DZ

An Hachette UK Company

www.hachette.co.uk

www.franklinwatts.co.uk

Contents

Who Was Turner?

Joseph Mallord William Turner was a British landscape painter, watercolour artist and printmaker. He is often known as "the painter of light" because of the brilliant colours he used in his **landscapes** and **seascapes**. He was born in 1775 at Maiden Lane, Covent Garden, in London.

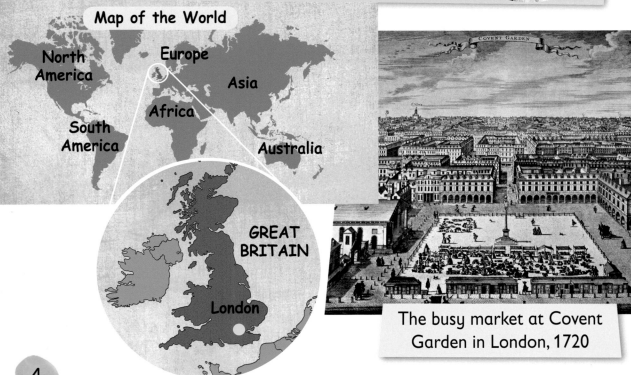

Map of the World

North America

Europe

Asia

Africa

South America

Australia

GREAT BRITAIN

London

The busy market at Covent Garden in London, 1720

Turner's father was a barber and wig maker. His mother was a butcher's daughter. Turner's younger sister died aged four, leaving him an only child. Turner's father encouraged his son's interest in art. He would display his son's artwork in the window of his barber shop!

Staying With Family

When he was ten, Turner went to stay with his uncle. Turner coloured in prints of landscapes while he was there. He became interested in art. A year later he visited Margate, a seaside town east of London. He did drawings of the buildings and countryside. Whenever Turner stayed with his uncle he would fill a sketchbook with drawings and watercolours.

A watercolour of St John's Church, Margate, painted when Turner was around 12 years old

Learning His Trade

Covent Garden was a busy area of London. Many people passed by his father's barber shop and saw Turner's paintings. At 12 years old, Turner was making money colouring prints. He started working with the **engraver** and artist Thomas Malton, drawing buildings and maps.

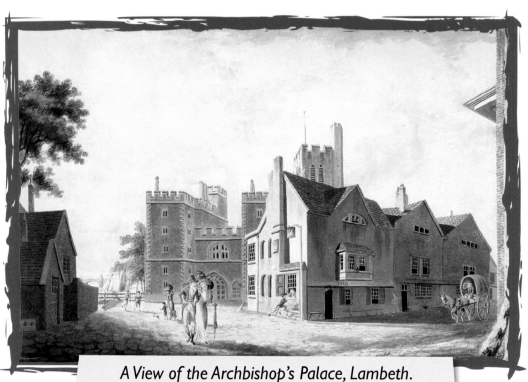

A View of the Archbishop's Palace, Lambeth.
This watercolour went in the Royal Academy's exhibition when Turner was just 15 years old!

A member of the Royal Academy of Arts noticed his paintings while having his hair cut. He was impressed with Turner's work and introduced him to the Royal Academy art school. Turner was accepted at the school when he was 15 years old.

7

The First Oil

Turner's watercolours hung at the school's famous exhibitions every year. In 1796, Turner had his first oil painting, *Fishermen at Sea*, below, accepted by the Royal Academy.

Prints Make Money

Turner earned money to help pay for his tuition by drawing engravings. He did designs for magazines. He also made copies of unfinished drawings by other artists. Their work inspired Turner and his **etchings** got better and better.

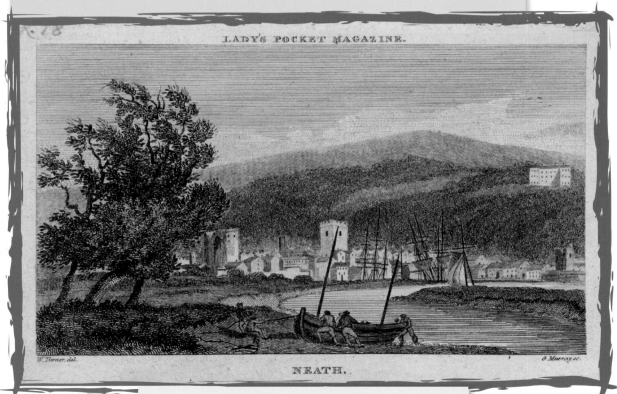

Neath, 1795. This drawing by Turner was published in the *Lady's Pocket Magazine*.

Turner began to travel to find inspiration for his pictures. A war in Europe meant that he travelled in Britain at first. He made his first trip to Europe in 1802, during a gap in the war with France. Switzerland's mountains and lakes inspired him.

Lake Thun

Turner visited Lake Thun in the Swiss Alps on his first tour in 1802. He made many pencil sketches of the lake in a sketchbook. Turner later did a watercolour of the same scene. Can you spot any changes to the figures in the painting below?

Becoming Successful

Turner's growing popularity led him to open a gallery at his new home in London. Turner exhibited watercolours done from drawings from his European tour.

The new gallery was a much better space than the crowded Academy gallery. It attracted some new customers. Walter Fawkes became a collector of his work, and became a close friend. Turner often stayed at his home, Farnley Hall.

Chamonix and Mont Blanc from the Path to the Montenvers, 1802. Many of Turner's paintings have faded over time. This painting would have had a blue sky and much greener trees.

No Money In The Bank

Even though Turner was earning a good deal of money, he never had a bank account. Turner bought houses and **shares** in companies with his money instead.

The Dort Packet-Boat from Rotterdam Becalmed, 1818. This very precise style was typical of Turner's early paintings.

A Divided Year

Turner would travel and sketch in the summer. When he was back in his studio in the winter he would use the sketches to help him create his paintings.

House Guest

Turner often stayed at friends' houses to paint. Turner had some wealthy friends! He stayed at the Earl of Egremont's estate, Petworth House.

Petworth, Sussex, the Seat of the Earl of Egremont: Dewy Morning, 1810

Turner's mother became mentally ill after the death of her daughter. She went to live in a hospital, and Turner's father came to live with him. He worked as Turner's assistant and helped to sell his paintings.

Keelmen Heaving in Coals by Moonlight, 1835

Painting the Weather

Turner liked to paint the effects of weather. *Calais Pier*, below, was created after Turner had taken his first trip abroad to Calais, France. The sea was very rough. The dark sailboat full of people in the centre would have been his ferry. The painting was criticised. People thought it looked unfinished!

Calais Pier, 1803

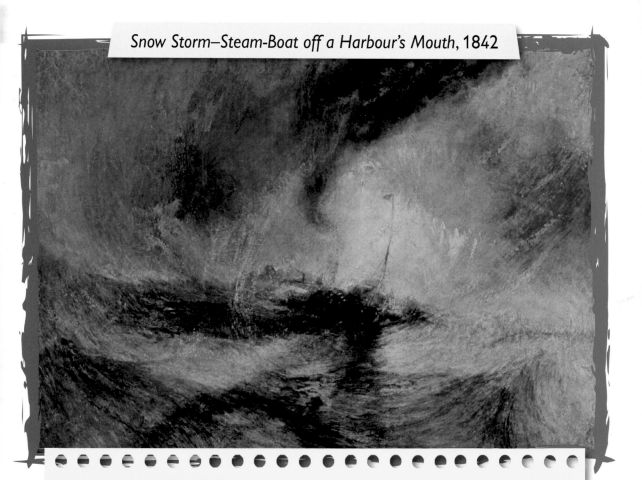

Snow Storm—Steam-Boat off a Harbour's Mouth, 1842

Experiencing the Storm

Turner went to great lengths to get the right emotions into this painting, called *Snow Storm*. Turner asked to be tied to a ship's mast during a storm, so that he could experience what it was like! The painting really gives you the feeling of what it would be like in a storm at sea. You wouldn't be able to see very much detail!

The Fighting Temeraire

Turner's most famous painting is probably
The Fighting Temeraire. Painted in 1839, it shows
a famous warship's last journey to the scrapyard.

The Warship

The ship, HMS *Temeraire*, was used during a great sea battle against France and Spain. The ship was one of the Royal Navy's most famous warships. Turner kept the painting in his studio and refused to sell it.

Turner lived during the **industrial revolution**. This was a time when many new things were invented. The steam ship was taking over from the sail ship. In this picture the new little steam-driven tugboat represents the future. The old sailing ship represents the past. Most people don't think it is a sad painting, though. The new tough little tug boat is a sign that there will be a powerful, exciting future.

The painting's full title is *The Fighting Temeraire tugged to her last berth to be broken up.*

17

Painting Trains

When Turner was born, people travelled by stagecoach. During his lifetime, the new railways changed transport for ever. In the 1840s a train moving at around 60 miles (96.5 km) per hour was an amazing sight.

Turner began to use oil paint more like watercolour, using **transparent** washes of colour. He liked painting light and movement. The painting *Rain, Steam and Speed* is a good example of this **technique**. The train and bridges are hard to make out. This is not a painting of a train, but a painting of the effect of a train.

Rain, Steam and Speed. The Great Western Railway, 1844.

Painter of Light

Turner painted this picture of Rome ten years after his last trip to the city. It was painted at the height of his career from sketches made on his two visits to the city. The light from a warm Italian late afternoon seems to shimmer in the picture.

Moon and Sun

When this painting was first shown at the Royal Academy, Turner put a line from a poem by Lord Byron next to it. "The moon is up, and yet it is not night, The sun as yet divides the day with her." Turner wanted the light effects of the sunset and the moon in his painting. The orb in the center is the moon.

Modern Rome—Campo Vaccino, 1839.
In 2010 this painting was sold for a record amount for a Turner picture. The Getty Museum paid £29.7 million for the work!

Turner and Venice

Turner made many visits to Venice, Italy. Venice is famous for its canals. The buildings seem to float on the water. The sun reflects off the water with a shimmering light. The city inspired Turner to create some of his best paintings.

The Grand Canal, Venice, 1835

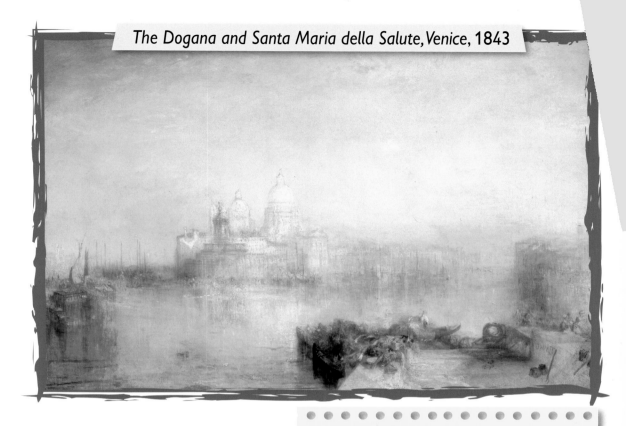

The Dogana and Santa Maria della Salute, Venice, 1843

With its water, weather and light, Venice was the perfect place for Turner to paint. His buildings were not that accurate, though. The tower in *The Grand Canal* painting is much taller than it really is. What is accurate is the atmosphere and light.

A Romantic

Turner was a Romantic painter. Romantic painters use imagination, emotion and expression in their work. In his paintings of Venice, Turner did not just record how the city looked, but added his own romantic impression of it.

Sunsets and Disasters

A little like a modern news photographer, Turner recorded disasters such as fires and shipwrecks in his work. Turner himself watched the burning of the Houses of Parliament as it happened. He made sketches using pencil and watercolour from different places, including from a rented boat!

The Burning of the Houses of Parliament, 1835. Turner painted the drama, flames and smoke. People watched from the riverbank and boats.

The Evening of the Deluge, 1843. Turner painted the Bible story of Noah and the flood. You can see the rain approaching as Noah and his wife lie in their tent.

Volcanoes and Sunsets

In 1816, a huge volcano **erupted** in Indonesia. The ash in the air led to spectacular sunsets for years afterward. These sunsets inspired much of Turner's work.

Mount Tambora, Indonesia.

A Matter of Taste

Some critics thought Turner's paintings were too pale, or lacked detail. Turner's **personality** did not always make him friends, either. He could be quite rude. He had a strong London accent, and was described as looking a little like a farmer! Some people in the art world disliked him because of it.

Turner's house and gallery fell into ruin. Visitors described it as having grimy windows and leaks in the roof. If it rained, visitors apparently needed an umbrella while they looked around!

Secret Life

For many years Turner lived with a woman, Sophia Booth, in a house by the river. He called himself Admiral Booth. Everyone thought that they were married, and that he was a seaman. No one knew he was the famous J.M.W. Turner!

Staffa, Fingal's Cave, 1832

The American collector James Lenox wanted to own a Turner painting. But he bought one without having seen it first! Lenox's friend chose *Staffa, Fingal's Cave* for him. Lenox had only seen Turner's etchings before. His friend was worried he may not like the painting. He was right! Lenox said the painting was **indistinct**. Turner replied "indistinctness is my **forte**!"

A Royal Academy Legacy

Turner exhibited for the last time at the Royal Academy in 1850. He was always a strong supporter of the Academy and always enjoyed "Varnishing Day". This was the day before the exhibition opened, when the artists could meet, and make finishing touches to their work.

The Red Buoy

Rival artist John Constable's colourful painting hung next to Turner's paler painting, *Helvoetsluys*, on Varnishing Day. Worried, Turner added a red buoy to his own **canvas**. This bright red mark completely took attention away from Constable's painting!

Turner on Varnishing Day, William Parrott, 1846. Turner would add last minute touches to his paintings.

Turner died in 1851 aged 76. His last words were said to be "The Sun is God". He was buried in St Paul's Cathedral, London. Turner influenced the **Impressionist** and **Post-Impressionist** painters that came after him. He is believed to be the greatest British landscape painter. Turner left a large amount of money to the Royal Academy to help struggling artists. He also left hundreds of paintings and drawings to the British nation.

Glossary

canvas
A piece of cloth used as a surface for painting.

engraver
Someone who cuts or carves letters or designs.

erupted
To burst forth or explode.

etchings
Prints made from an etched metal plate.

forte The thing a person does very well, a strong point.

Impressionist
An artist who concentrates on the impression of a scene using unmixed primary colours and small brush strokes to simulate light.

indistinct
Not distinct or clear.

industrial revolution
A period during which power-driven machinery was introduced.

landscapes
Pictures of the natural scenery.

personality
The emotions and
behaviour that make a
person different.

Post Impressionist
An artist who reacted
against the naturalism of
the impressionists.

seascapes
Picture of a scene at sea.

shares
Equal portions of a
business that people own.

technique
A method of achieving a
desired aim.

transparent
Able to be seen through.

Websites

A Tate Kids site which lets you create some Turner masterpieces
http://kids.tate.org.uk/games/discovering-turner/

BBC website with a slideshow of all Turner's best paintings
http://www.bbc.co.uk/arts/yourpaintings/artists/joseph-mallord-william-turner

Every effort has been made by the publisher to ensure that these
websites contain no inappropriate or offensive material. However,
because of the nature of the Internet, it is impossible to guarantee
that the content of these sites will not be altered. We strongly
advise that Internet access is supervised by a responsible adult.

Read More

Kramer, Ann. *Artists*. Great Britons. London, UK: Franklin Watts, 2007.

Mayhew, James. *Katie and the British Artists*. London, UK: Orchard Books, 2009.

Thomson, Leo. *Place and Space*. Landscapes in Art (Artventure). London: Wayland, 2005.

Index